THE HORROR OF HANNITY
© 2016 BY PAUL COVELL

Table of Contents

Foreword

Politics in the U.S. and most countries never equated with bean ball. In the beginning of our Nation, few objected to the election of George Washington to the Presidency. Partisans fought fierce battles over election of all other presidents. The First President counseled against factions, later known as political parties. Before the birth of the U.S., the British Colonies in America banded together as United Colonies. The struggle whether to form a united country in 1789 revolved over the degree of power the Sovereign Independent States would willingly cede to the nascent central Government.

Federalists and Anti-Federalists fought a propaganda war to win the hearts and minds of their compatriots. Alexander Hamilton, James Madison, and John Jay wrote essays called the Federalist Papers. States Rights' supporters such as James Winthrop of Massachusetts and Patrick Henry and George Mason of Virginia highlighted the danger of giving power to the national government. The battle continues to this day between States' Rights versus the power of the federal government. Mason would rather cut off his hand than put it to the Constitution as written.

Leadership of the Nation reserved for the best minds and hearts. Selecting leaders fell to the American People under the Constitution. Putting leaders up for election fell to the power brokers. Cigar-smoking kingmakers met in smoke filled hotel rooms to decide which candidate to present to the People. Party Leaders and influential business owners led the way by coalescing around the most winsome candidate. George W. Bush comes to mind.

Some candidates forced their way onto the scene. Ronald Reagan comes to mind. Coalescing under the leadership of party bosses seemed undemocratic until the GOP Steeplechase of 2016. The race was wide open until the least serious candidate proved unstoppable in the Republican primaries.

Donald Trump insulted and bullied all of his primary opponents. The GOP Base loved it. Tea Party Members of Congress came to Washington to overturn the old order. Trump could be a Chief Executive who would tear down the Washington Establishment. Trump was not a Conservative. He was not even a Republican. Self-respecting Conservatives and Republicans ran away from the GOP nominee. Trump flailed about, changing Campaign Managers three times in a desperate attempt to right a sinking ship.

How could Trump hang on in the face of withering criticism with- in and without the conservative establishment? The answer is *The Horror of Hannity* enabled Trump to hang on long after facts showed he was unfit to serve.

Right Wing Talk Shows exist to smear the Democrat and to extol the Republican candidate, no matter what. Rupert Murdoch offered to buy the Cable News Network (CNN) in the 90s. Ted Turner rejected the offer. Murdoch commissioned Roger Ailes to create a network that would compete with CNN and appeal to the business community. Thus, Fox News Network came into existence. Fox promised *Fair and Balanced* treatment of the news of the day. Fox, however, rigged the show featuring Alan Combes and Sean Hannity to allow Hannity to prevail.

Hannity reportedly makes $22 million a year as the defender of Republicans and the reflexive critic of Democrats. After shadow boxing for a couple of years, Alan Combes went to pasture. Hannity became Champion of Republican Causes. Roger Ailes stepped down as Fox News Chair in August 2016, possibly to allow more time to defend against sexual harassment claims.

Hannity is the darling of the GOP *'Pay to Play'* Crowd. Rudy Giuliani loves to come on Hannity to spread smears concocted by *Breitbart News and Views from the Dark Side*. As the wheels came off the Trump Campaign Train, Rudy came up with a gem. It does not matter if Trump is unfit, Hillary Clinton is visibly not well according to the boys in the fever swamp.

Hannity Broadcast a video snippet of Hillary bobbing her head in a *'give me a break response'* to a flurry of reporters' questions. Hannity concluded that Hillary had a stroke on camera. Rudy Giuliani concurred. Better to have an unfit misogynist with a racial attitude than a progressive bobble head dedicated to public service. It shows how desperate Fox News is be *'Fair and Balanced'* in favor of a

GOP nominee, who is dying from self-inflicted wounds. Drudge and Breitbart rumors about Hillary's health turned out to have some factual basis, as will be seen.

The *Horror of Hannity* shows up on myriad radio and TV shows that are also fair—and balanced *precariously* on the Right Wing of political extremism. As the Trump Campaign lurches into the abyss, it seems as though P.T. Barnum is writing the script. Are we all dreaming, or did Donald Trump really introduce Nigel Farage at a Trump Rally? Farage was leader of the UK Independent Party in the successful and stressful (*Brexit*) vote to leave the European Union.

Trump supporters had no idea of who Farage is, or why he appeared on stage with Trump. The *Horror of Hannity* is that Hannity would conclude that the bizarre scene showed Trump's grasp of international relations. It was just another Trump publicity stunt and photo op.

Conventional wisdom is that Trump will launch his own TV network in 2017. He never wanted to be president.

Chapter 1
Cable News War Zone

Have you ever wondered why News today generally presents as *'Breaking News'?* There is nothing staler than stale news. If it is not *'breaking'*, by definition, it is not new, and, thus, not newsworthy. In the *'Pay to Play'* world we live in, sponsors pay extra for extra viewers. There is a ratio of dollars payable per pop. The competition among Cable News is for advertising dollars. Fox News caters to a conservative audience.

The GOP Party Line is the *'Fair and Balanced'* potion specially brewed by Fox for a conservative audience. It is like having Colmes and Hannity filtered to eliminate progressive ideas. Fox News is the **propaganda arm** of the Republican Party. *The Horror of Hannity* is that we already know what Hannity will say in any given context. Hannity will say whatever is necessary to advance the Republican cause. The problem is that the Republican Party is not in harmony with the conservative cause. The GOP in 2016 is a plaything of Donald Trump.

Trump won the GOP primaries in 2016 by stirring up racial animosity. This is not a new tactic for Republicans. The GOP generates *'fire in the belly'* through appealing to the aspirations of millions of disaffected Democrats, who fled to the GOP as *'social conservatives'*. Strom Thurmond (R-SC) did not want to get into bed with those he held inferior, except for brief flirtations.

Strom stormed out of the 1948 Democratic Convention in protest to a civil rights platform. This was 17 years before Lyndon Johnson signed the *Voting Rights Act of 1965* into law. Thurmond saw the direction taken by the Democrats. Thurmond knew that Civil Rights would inevitably lead to voting rights for African Americans nearly 100 years after adoption of the 13th, 14th, and 15th Amendments to the U.S. Constitution.

That Thurmond mellowed his racial stand in middle age is a credit to his ability to develop. He is the only person ever elected in modern times to the U.S. Senate by Write-in-Vote. The majority of the electorate in South Carolina knew where Thurmond stood.

Chapter 2
Fanning the Flames

The *Horror of Hannity* is that animosity and racial division sell. Antagonism earns big bucks for professional potboilers like Hannity. Trump and Hannity are interested in policy only as a means to fan the flames of discontent and bigotry. Trump has no core policies, but he fakes policies to gin up support of the GOP Base. Trump claimed he wanted to deport 11 million undocumented workers. Hannity, Anne Coulter, and Rush Limbaugh applauded. Trump realized the impracticality of mass deportations, and softened his ever-changing position in late August 2016.

Hannity, Coulter, and Limbaugh threw a fit. GOP activists need someone to dislike. Republicans want to take our country back. Trump wants to go back to the good old days of the 50s and 60's, when Orval Faubus was Governor of Arkansas and George (segregation forever) Wallace ran Alabama.

Republicans do not like the *Voting Rights Act of 1965* and its progeny. Republicans know that Democrats generally prevail whenever the voter turnout is high, Ronald Reagan's wins in 1980 and '84 being the exception. Enterprising Republicans like Rick Scott, Governor of Florida, have programs to remove voters from eligible lists. Those removed from voting rolls somehow turn out to be mostly Democrats.

GOP minority monitors will challenge minority voters to discourage voting. Governor Scott also can hold down the vote by cutting resources to Democratic Counties. Miami-Dade comes to mind. If there are not enough voting machines, minority voters may not be able to wait in line for six hours. The State of Oregon has used voting by mail exclusively for years with great success. Democracy requires more citizen participation, not less.

Negative Campaigning causes voter apathy and cynicism. When Trump says, **'the system is rigged'**, that is a **dog whistle** for the GOP Base, which mistrusts Government. If Trump wins the election, we lose because

Trump is not fit temperamentally to be president. If Trump loses the election, we suffer harm because Trump will say the system is rigged. Trump and the *Horror of Hannity* are harmful because they breed apathy and cynicism. Once the American People distrust the federal, state and local government, citizen participation in civic affairs declines.

Voter turnout follows the pessimism on a downward glide path. Suspicion and skepticism form a double helix in a downward spiral. Fewer and fewer voters control the political destiny of the Nation. Simple majority vote determines an election

If only 50% of eligible voters show up on Election Day, control is in the hands of 25%, plus 1 vote. The situation is more alarming as voter turnout falls below 50%. You do the math for a 30% voter turnout. There is no excuse for not voting, when absentee ballots are freely available. The U.S. may need an award of $10 for voting and a penalty of $10 for unexcused failure to vote.

Republicans, however, are not that civic minded when it comes to encouraging the masses to vote. The bottom of the pyramid in the 21st century tends to vote for the progressive ticket, usually represented by Democrats. Bernie Sanders (I-VT) is a progressive Independent, who caucuses with the Democrats. Republicans fear that if 100% of eligible voters turn out, the Democrats will win. Therefore, the GOP tries to suppress the vote.

Republicans cannot admit they are playing a numbers game, i. e., keeping the number of voters low, so the Republicans will win. GOP propagandists will always say that they are trying to purify the vote, and keep it sacred. Rick Scott, Republican Governor of Florida, claimed he was only eliminating criminals from the voter rolls. If your name was Gonzales, however, there was more of a chance

Governor Scott would remove your name from the voter rolls than if your name was Bush.

Contrast Rick Scott's approach with that of Terry McAuliffe, Democratic Governor of the State of Virginia. Convicted felons were not allowed to vote in Virginia. Governor McAuliffe supported a bill to allow rehabilitation of those convicted of some lesser felonies, so they could vote. Republicans represent the money class. Republicans fear the base of the pyramid. The only felons the GOP would want to vote are white collar criminals, who would make more than $75,000 upon release from prison.

The *Horror of Hannity* is that Hannity supports GOP vote suppression, but under a more euphemistic name of course.

Donald Trump made a calculated political choice in 2016. He decided to employ a bottom up strategy instead of top down. He wanted to appeal to the masses, the man and woman in the street, if you will. He is not chasing Anne Romney. He feels that the upper 1% are with him at all events. Trump's *hoi polloi* strategy came apart at the seams, however. He wore his baseball cap to convince ordinary folks that he is one of them. What demography supports him? Competing factions, who want opposing policies, limit him.

He has been courting Hispanic Leaders. He even flew to Mexico City to meet President Peña. He could not waffle any longer on immigration. The GOP Base wants to deport 11 million undocumented workers. Trump announced that he would be moderate on a path to citizenship, and then that illegals would have to leave, go back to their own country, and apply for a U.S. visa. Hispanic Leaders felt betrayed. Because Trump has run a rude, crude campaign, many who generally vote Republican will not vote for him.

In a desperate gamble, Trump is visiting African American Churches.

On September 17, 2016. Trump met with a group in Texas that lost family members to murder by illegal immigrants. CNN televised part of the event, but Admission was limited to those approved by the Trump campaign. Trump used his usual wedge issue tactics to seek to stir up racial and ethnic animosity. Trump told his usual dozen lies, and, of course, claimed that Hillary Clinton wanted an open border despite the risk of crime.

Trump misrepresented most of Hillary's policies on immigration. Studies have shown consistently that immigrants do not commit more crime than native born citizens of the U.S. Trump has such a reputation as a pathological liar that few believe him anymore. Hillary Clinton does not favor allowing admission of dangerous criminals across an open border. Hillary used the term *'open borders'* in a speech in connection with trade and sharing energy resources. Republicans went wild in denouncing open borders.

The issue facing Hillary and progressives is what to do about millions of undocumented workers, who have families, have paid taxes, and are law abiding residents of the U.S. Massive deportation is impractical. What happens to families that have children born in the U.S?

Trump's pandering to both sides has not presented any answers. He promises Hispanic Leaders that he will deport criminal immigrants, but will wait and see what to do about immigrants who are undocumented but are not criminals. He promises his base that all undocumented workers will have to return to their country of origin and apply for U.S. visas.

Even Kellyanne Conway cannot make Trump's pandering and lies palatable. Kellyanne was supposed to make Trump acceptable to women, but his confession of sexual harassment and groping of women, disclosed on tape on the Access Hollywood bus ride, made Trump a pariah.

Chapter 3
GOP: Grand Old Wedge Party

Donald Trump looked as though he was a supporter of Bernie Sanders during the Democratic Primary. Sanders complained that the Democratic National Committee (DNC) rigged the primary in favor of Hillary. Trump was sympathetic. He offered to debate Sanders to give the underdog more visibility. This was standard GOP strategy to look for daylight between two groups, and drive a wedge between them.

It should not come as a surprise that long term staffers at DNC favored the long term Democrat over the Independent challenger. The DNC Chair should have imposed impartiality. She did not. So, she had to go. What is surprising is that Trump has not made that much of the standard wedge issues that the GOP generally relies upon.

It appears that Trump is a supporter of *Right to Life*, but he seemed to support a woman's *Right to Choose* in the past. The latest wedge issue the GOP dredged up is the hysteria over bathroom privileges for transgender folks. If a person is born a male, and switches to female, can that person use the Ladies Room? The GOP wants any doubt resolved by the person's birth certificate.

If a person was born male, Republican Wedge Issue Policy says that person can never enter the Ladies Room, transgender change or not. The Legislature of North

Carolina enacted a law to stop transgender folks from using the bathroom of transgender identification. A federal judge declared the law unconstitutional. At the GOP Convention, the only platform plank Trump looked at was to *remove* the promise to Keep NATO Strong. Vladimir Putin celebrated. Tony Perkins of the *American Family* took care of most of the other wedge issues at the Convention.

Trump's journey on immigration has been fascinating. During the GOP primaries, Trump went overboard in favor of a harsh immigration policy. Trump declared that he was building a wall on the southwest border to keep out Mexicans. He promised that Mexico would pay for the wall. Mexico demurred. Trump promised to deport 11 million undocumented workers. After the primaries, Trump looked at his Electoral Vote Computer. The count was dismal. He could not win if he took only 1% of the African American vote and 22% of the Hispanic Vote.

Trump waffled on immigration. He wanted to be humane. Rush Limbaugh and Anne Coulter were devastated. It sounded like **Amnesty**, which is dirty word to Republicans. Ronald Reagan sponsored amnesty in 1986. When he saw that he might lose the GOP Base, Trump went back to his position of mass deportation. In desperation, he started vising African American churches. He needed a minority group to support him.

Who said Trump would not pivot toward a general election campaign strategy? Trump's handlers have forced the bullyboy to pivot away from incessant incoherent tweets and rallies in front of base cheerleaders. During the week of September, Trump is dressing up, and posing presidential. Kellyanne Conway is making headway on transforming the sullen teenager into presidential timber. The cake, however, baked months ago. A majority of the

American people know that Trump is not fit to serve as president.

These desperate last ditch efforts to fool African Americans, Hispanics, and college educated whites, is doomed to failure. The pathetic effort of Jason Chaffetz (R-UT), Chair, Government Oversight, to persuade the Justice Department to prosecute the Democratic candidate likewise is doomed to failure. The Republicans have no solutions to the Nation's problems. Six years after passage of the *Affordable Care Act*, the Republicans have no plan but to denounce Obama's Plan, which was a Republican idea in the first place.

Chapter 4

Why Obama Mattered

Barack Obama was an unlikely choice for President in 2008. He had been in the U.S. Senate for only two years. He had no foreign policy credentials. He had no executive experience. He was a Community Organizer, an attorney, a part time Law Professor, and a former Member of the Illinois State Senate for a few years. When he ran against Bobby Rush (D-IL) for Congress, Rush whooped him badly. Obama had an eye for history, and he knew that George W. Bush made a mistake by advocating the Invasion of Iraq.

Many Democratic Senators voted for the 2003 Iraq War, including Hillary Clinton and John Kerry. Obama did not vote on the War in the U.S. Senate, because he was not there. Obama was a Senator in the Illinois State Senate. He did write an Op Ed piece declaring that he was not against all wars. He was against **Dumb Wars**. Obama thought the 2003 Iraq War was dumb.

Ironically, Vice President Dick Cheney at one time thought invading Iraq was *not* a good idea. Cheney was Secretary of Defense for Poppy Bush, when the U.S. pushed Saddam Hussein out of Kuwait in 1990-91. Cheney counseled against invading Iraq, because it would get us into a *"quagmire"* Cheney knew what he was talking about with respect to the 1990 War. He abandoned his good judgment in 2003 by going all in on the Invasion of Iraq.

The Harvard Law Review elected Law student Obama President of the Review. Obama's first job out of law school was with a law firm, where he met Michelle. Michelle mentored Barack on behalf of the law firm. After he reached the Illinois State Senate, Party Leaders took note, especially after his *'Dumb War'* article.

Dick Durbin (D-IL) was impressed. In 2008, the Democrats in the Senate had to choose between Hillary and Barack. Chuck Schumer was Senior Senator from New York, and supported Hillary, the junior Senator from New York. Durbin, Kerry, Joe Biden, and Senate Majority Leader Harry Reid supported Barack. Hillary ran a good campaign in states that held primaries. Barack won his fair share of primaries, but excelled in the caucus states. Hillary's vote in favor of the 2003 Iraq War doubtless contributed to her loss in 2008.

John McCain conducted an uneven campaign in 2008. At one point, when the money ran out, McCain fired most of his staff. He recovered financially, and his campaign hit stride again. Two things were a drag on McCain's campaign. Most viewed the 2003 Iraq War as an unmitigated disaster. Second, the U.S. economy fell apart. No one could get credit or borrow money. All the overnight funds that corporations and banks used to make available disappeared.

Lehman Brothers started as cotton brokers in Montgomery, Alabama in the 1850s. Lehman had six hundred billion in assets in 2008, but could not borrow three hundred million needed as operating capital to stay in business. Hank Paulson, Secretary of the Treasury, could not entice any major player to come to Lehman's rescue. Leman filed bankruptcy. Bank of America took over Countrywide Home Loans. Corporate America started a massive reduction in labor force.

By January 2009, there were 700,000 layoffs a month in corporate America. The Nation was in a severe recession. McCain never had a chance.

Obama won in 2008, and won re-election in 2012. If America was racist, it did not show. Republicans may complain that African Americans voted overwhelmingly for Barack Obama. What do they expect the result should be for the first African American presidential candidate?

Mitt Romney ran a good campaign in 2012 but appeared as a patrician. His business interests in the Cayman Islands did not help. Compared to the antics of Donald Trump in 2016, Romney's Race in 2012 looked flawless.

There was a gaffe at a fundraiser that was recorded by the catering staff. *'Forty Seven percent of voters will vote for Obama anyway'*, according to Romney. Romney thought those folks considered themselves **victims**. Forty-Seven turned into fifty-one, point one, but they were not victims. Romney took 47.2% of the Vote.

Chapter 5
Trump, Uniquely Unqualified

What makes the *Horror of Hannity* far worse is that Donald Trump is uniquely unqualified to be president.

Trump is the worst candidate fielded by the GOP in 167 years. Fred Trump and his son, Donald, had an aversion to African Americans, at least as tenants in Trump residential properties. The Department of Justice sued father and son for violation of the *Fair Housing Act.*

Donald reacted petulantly, and retained Roy Cohn, former counsel for Senator Joseph McCarthy's Committee that investigated communists in the government. Trump filed a counterclaim against the U.S. for defamation, and sought a restraining order. The Court did not grant Trump the relief requested. After a couple of years of thrashing about in litigation, Trump agreed to settle through a Consent Decree.

As customary, the Trump defendants did not admit any wrongdoing and promised to not violate *The Fair Housing Act* in the future.

As the director of his own reality show, Mr. Trump claimed victory. The Department of Justice had compelling evidence that the Trumps discriminated against African Americans. The Trump organization summarily rejected blacks' applications as residential tenants in a Trump property. Fred Trump instructed his manager to place one black tenant's application in a desk drawer, and leave it there indefinitely.

The Court later ordered Trump to rent to the woman, who noted that she was the only black in the property for many years. Trump's agent testified that Trump ordered him to attach to rental applications from African Americans a paper marked "C" for colored. Despite the Consent Decree, the Department of Justice discovered that Trump persisted in discriminating against Blacks.

The Trumps escaped a follow up enforcement action only because the government allowed the effective date of the Consent Decree to expire before bringing the follow up enforcement action. To this day, Trump seeks to avoid responsibility for housing discrimination by claiming that *he does not know* what some Building Superintendent might have done at a Trump apartment building.

In order conflate his discrimination, Trump accused Hillary of being a bigot. Trump's tenuous theory is that Hillary is a Democrat, Democrats control the big cities, and Black unemployment is high. Therefore, Hillary is allegedly is a bigot. Trump's arguments would not convince a fourth grader. The *Archie Bunker* crowd, however, believes in the Donald.

The most egregious offense committed by Trump against the body politic was his takeover of the delegitimization of the Nation's First Black President. Trump became **Birther-in-Chief** in 2011, vigorously advocating the lie that President Obama was not born in the U.S. Trump lied to the American People when he claimed that he sent investigators to Hawaii to uncover the evidence to show that the President's Birth Certificate is false.

It is apparent that Trump seriously considered campaigning for president for some time. Trump could see that Hillary Clinton, as Secretary of State, might be the Democratic nominee. What better way to topple Hillary than to cast Obama as an undocumented alien. The smear would work equally as well if Vice president Biden were the nominee. Trump's role as Birther-in-Chief was not a mistake of fact. Trump knew the facts. Trump knew that Obama was born in Hawaii, and he had no reason to doubt that fact.

Trump pandered to the crazies in the Republican Right Wing. Trump knew that any attack against President Obama would energize his Base, which would support

Trump vigorously in the 2016 Primary. It did not matter to the GOP Base if the attack was a smear or a lie. Trump's entire Presidential Campaign tried to exacerbate racial tension, and to appeal to the *Archie Bunker* Vote. Trump's anti American Campaign proves that Trump is not fit to be Commander-in-Chief.

On September 16, 2016, after five years of slurs against President Obama's birthplace, **Trump caved**. He admitted President Obama was born in the U.S.A. To avoid losing more face after conceding the truth, Trump slunk away from the microphone—and refused to take questions from reporters. Trump's five year smear campaign against the President's legitimacy proved to be a fraud. Trump can call off the mythical investigators he supposedly sent to Hawaii to uncover the evidence of Obama's allegedly false birth certificate.

How much proof do the American people need that Donald Trump is a huckster, who will say anything to try be elected? **The Horror of Hannity** is that Hannity and the other talking Heads give Trump a pass on Trump's smears and racially divisive campaign tactics.

His attacks on Judge Curiel and the Khan Family only confirm his lack of fitness to be president. Trump desperately wants to see dismissal of the lawsuit against Trump University. Judge Curiel is an outstanding jurist, who was born in Indiana. His parents are Mexican. The judge presides over the Class Action lawsuit against Trump University. Trump promised to build a wall between Mexico and the U.S. Trump accused the judge of prejudice in favor of plaintiffs in the suit because of Trump's threat to build a wall.

The Khan Family lost their son in action in Iraq in 2004. At the Democratic Convention, Khisr Khan criticized

Trump for his promise to ban Moslems from the U.S. until America can find out what is going on. Trump and his surrogates lashed out against the Khan Family. The Donald wanted to know why Mrs. Khan did not speak at the Democratic Convention.

Politics allows for petty grievances and minor fits of religious and racial animosity. When a candidates' entire campaign, however, depends on nothing but lies and religious and racial animosity, that campaign will implode without just and reasonable policies to give it structure and purpose. Trump has no discernible policy, other than that he wants to win. If winning requires lying, then Trump is all-in on lying.

If it will help Trump to say that President Obama is not an American citizen, then Trump will do it. If it will help to smear Hillary Clinton, Trump will do it. Trump staged his Convention to win. Trump recruited Pat Smith, mother of Sean Smith, killed by terrorists at the U.S. Mission at Benghazi, Libya, to blame Hillary for the death of Sean. Trump knows that Hillary Clinton did not cause the death of Sean Smith.

Trump has no regard for facts or the truth. Trump respects only winning, and he will try to do whatever it takes to avoid losing.

The *Horror of Hannity* is that we have lost our Nation to a corrupt Republican Party and the propagandists who preach the Party Line. The *Land of the Brave* and the *Home of the Free* is a bazaar for *Pay to Play* GOP opportunists, who will do anything to control the White House. Hannity has no more respect for the truth than does Trump. The Trump Campaign is a hoax. GOP Leadership is embarrassed to have Trump as nominee.

African American support for Trump is at 1%. Hispanic support for Trump is less than 22%. Support for Trump by educated women is less than 30%. The *Horror of Hannity* is that Hannity makes millions by lying for Trump. We know that Hannity will continue to lie to try to pull Trump's campaign out of the abyss. The lower Trump sinks in the polls, the more lies Hannity will tell. Desperation motivates Hannity to broadcast rumors of Hillary's imagined poor health. Hannity has nowhere else to go, because Trump is a loser. Trump is not qualified to be president.

On 9/11/16, Hillary left the 9/11 memorial ceremony early, obviously feeling ill. The doctor diagnosed pneumonia and recommended a week's rest. Republicans see this as a chance for Trump to win. It would be ironic if the unqualified candidate won because the qualified candidate fell sick temporarily. Everyone is subject to occasional sickness. Rest will probably help.

The Democratic Party is taking Hillary's illness seriously. If Hillary were unable to continue (which is not the case), the Democrats would have to come up with a substitute candidate for president. The present VP candidate, Tim Kaine, is the likely choice. What would happen if the Party called upon Joe Biden to continue his public service? It is unlikely that Biden would want to sign on for another four years as Vice President.

Would Kaine, however, agree to the choice of Biden at the top of the ticket? There are no rules on the procedure to find a replacement after the disability of the presidential candidate. Time is of the essence. The states will have to order ballots printed in October. 2016 promises to be an unusual election year, if only because of the presence of Donald Trump.

All the handwringing over Hillary's emails is overblown. Hillary made a mistake by using a home server for State Department email. Bill Clinton had a server at their Chappaqua, N.Y. home. Hillary thought it would be convenient to use the home server. That was a mistake. Because Hillary was Secretary of State, there was no one in a position of authority at State to inform Hillary that she could not use a home server for State business.

After Hillary left State, the Inspector General raised the issue of the home server, and, ultimately, referred the question to Justice. After a thorough investigation, FBI Director James Comey announced that he found no prosecutable offense in Hillary's handling of State Department email.

Since Trump is a loser by personality, Republicans chafed at the failure of the FBI to take Hillary out of the 2016 presidential race. Jason Chaffetz (R-UT), Chair of the House Committee for Government Oversight and Reform, held a Hearing. Director Comey stated that no reasonable prosecutor would bring a case against Hillary for email security violations. Rudy Giuliani disagreed.

Desperate to disqualify Hillary on some ground, Chaffetz asked Comey if Hillary transgressed by allegedly lying to Congress. Comey informed Chaffetz that the FBI would need a written referral. Chaffetz said, *"You will have one in a few hours."* The legislative branch is desperate to convince the executive branch to prosecute the Democratic candidate for president to pave the way for a self absorbed narcissist to win the presidency.

The Trump Campaign looks like a series of episodes of the *'Keystone Kops'*. Trump is the worst nominee in GOP history. Trump has no policies, other than to throw red meat to the GOP Base. Trump's ban on Moslems and proposed deportation of 11 million undocumented Hispanics fired up the Base. Trump defeated 16 contenders in the GOP primaries.

Trump realized that what turned on the GOP base would lose with Moslems, African Americans, Hispanics, and college educated women. Trump canceled a rally set for August 25 in Colorado to explain his Immigration policy. Trump knew he had no policy. Trump's immigration plan was softening, and then hardening. Trump asked an audience, *Should the U.S. deport or not.* The audience favored deportation. Trump's Campaign desperately asked Rush Limbaugh to support softening of the deportation plan. Rush laughed on the air.

In the meantime, Jason Chaffetz and Trey Gowdy (R-SC) are frantically looking for a way to disqualify Hillary. Gowdy chaired the Select Committee to investigate (for the ninth time) the attack on the U.S. Mission at Benghazi, Libya. Majority Leader Kevin McCarthy (R-CA) bragged that the Republicans ordered the investigation to bring down Hillary's poll numbers. John Boehner designated McCarthy as Speaker upon Boehner's retirement. McCarthy's admission about the GOP conspiracy to bring down Hillary's poll numbers cost McCarthy the Speaker's Gavel.

Paul Ryan came to the aid of the GOP once again, amnd agreed to serve as Speaker. Hillary testified for 11 hours. Gowdy never proved Hillary negligent for the terrorist attack on Benghazi, or culpable for the lack of response by the U.S. Military. The *Horror of Hannity* is that Republicans keep trying to smear Democratic candidates, and Hannity, Limbaugh, and the Right Wing Talk Shows support the GOP smears.

Who said Trump lacks international experience? Trump had Nigel Farage, Leader of UKIP, (United Kingdom Independent Party) and Brexit advocate, speak at a Rally. On 8/31/16, Trump traveled to Mexico to speak with President Peña. Mexicans are angry that Trump accused Mexico of sending criminals and rapists to the U.S. Trump angered the Government of Mexico by taunting that Mexico will pay for the wall he promised to build. The meeting in Mexico is curious. Trump's only strategy had to be to say that he was joking, and that his Mexico rants were just plain bull. Otherwise, there is no explanation for Trump's rude, crude behavior.

If Trump explains to the President of Mexico that his rants were just bull, he owes the American People the same explanation. We all know that Trump's Campaign is nothing but bull, but he should admit it anyway. The *Horror of Hannity* is that Hannity will try to find a way to justify Trump's bizarre Campaign.

Hannity has joined Trump in the fuzzy world of bull, as recently explained by Lawrence O'Donnell on the *Last Word*. If Hannity were a mere liar, we could ferret out the lies from the truth and half-truths. By interlacing his lies with bull, Hannity has made it more difficult to see where truth ends and lies begin. Because Hannity intentionally blurs the line between truth and bull, we must disbelieve everything he says.

When Hannity and Trump say Hillary is a bigot, they have two purposes in mind. First, to destroy the meaning of the word *'bigot'*. Second, to insulate Trump, the true bigot, from accusations founded in fact.

Chapter 6
He Kept Us Safe—*Really?*

Have you ever noticed how Hannity and Rudy Giuliani continually praise George W. Bush? *"He Kept Us Safe",* GOP apologists claim. **Really?** Did 9/11 happen on September 11, 2001? Was Bush sworn in on January 20, 2001? The Report by the Commission on the 9/11 Attack concluded that the intelligence system was **'blinking red'** in the summer of 2001. The CIA alerted Bush to imminent danger of attack on America by al Qaeda in the summer of 2001. Bush went to his ranch in Crawford, Texas, in August despite intelligence briefings that warned of an imminent attack on U.S. soil. The CIA delivered a Daily Brief to the President on intelligence of threats to U.S. interests.

*"The headline of a June 30 briefing to top officials was stark: 'Bin Ladin Planning High-Profile Attacks. *** [CIA Director] Tenet told us that in his world 'the system was blinking red'. ***The result was an article in the August 6 Presidential Daily Brief Titled: 'Bin Ladin Determined to Strike in U.S.' "*-**9/11 Report** at pp 254-260.

The Horror of Hannity is that the GOP Propaganda Machine confuses the issue in an attempt to convince the American People that the Republicans kept the country safe. The truth is that the Republicans did not keep us safe on 9/11. After the attack, which happened on the Bush-Cheney watch, Bush gratuitously dragged the U.S. into a needless war in Iraq in 2003. Bush, a former Air National Guard Pilot, assembled the most dangerous combination of actors possible to lead his Administration.

Bush was the swaggering Chief Executive and Texas Air National Guard Pilot, who was burning to avenge the 9/11 Attack. Cheney never served in the military, was the alleged adult on the team, and was embarrassed that he and his boy got a black eye on 9/11. Cheney quickly came up with the idea of preemptive attack on potential enemies.

Do not wait until a threat develops into an attack. The U.S. must attack first, according to Cheney. It is the same strategy recommended by Kim, Jong Un, dictator of North Korea. Defense Secretary Rumsfeld (a combat Navy Pilot) was a self-appointed genius, who thought he could take on Iraq with an invasion force of 50,000 U.S. troops.

Under Secretary of Defense Paul Wolfowitz was the theoretical brain behind the Iraq War. Wolfowitz never wore the uniform of the U.S. military.

Douglas Feith was Wolfowitz' Deputy. Feith never wore the uniform of the U.S. Feith was Head of *Special Plans* at the Pentagon. There was only one operational *Special Plan*, the Plan to Invade Iraq. **Wolfowitz and Feith wrote the Plan to Invade Iraq in 1992 for Defense Secretary Cheney** when Poppy Bush was President. Professional soldiers disagreed with Rumsfeld's proposed Light Invasion Force.

Eric Shinseki was a combat veteran. He wore Four Stars on his uniform. He was Army Chief of Staff. Shinseki estimated that the invasion *and* occupation of Iraq would require **several hundreds of thousands of troops**. Wolfowitz, the amateur civilian, ruled that Shinseki's estimate of troop levels needed to take over Iraq was *"wildly off the mark"*.

Rumsfeld allowed Shinseki to finish his term as Army Chief of Staff, but studiously ignored the General after the criticism of the level of force required to defeat Saddam *and* occupy Iraq.

The 2003 Invasion of Iraq Was Inevitable
From Election Day 2000

In one sense, the Attack on 9/11 triggered the 2003 Invasion of Iraq. That is a myth. The Attack on 9/11 *delayed* the Invasion of Iraq. There had to be a token bombing of Afghanistan and skirmishes with bin Laden's rebels first, as retribution for the Taliban's refusal to hand over Osama bin Laden. Bush was always going to invade Iraq. Wolfowitz wrote the Iraq Invasion Plan *nine years before 9/11.*

The Bush Administration was an amalgam of Christian Militants and Neoconservatives, all of whom wanted to flex their muscle in the Middle East. The neocons had Iraq in their crosshairs for a long time.

"In January 1998, the Project for a New American Century, an advocacy group for an Interventionist Republican foreign policy, issued a letter urging President Clinton to take 'regime change' in Iraq seriously."-**Fiasco** by Thomas E. Ricks, (Penguin 2006) at p. 17.

After the military explained that there were no attractive bombing targets left in Afghanistan in 2003, the Bush Administration turned its sights back to the main target, Iraq. Bush asked Tenet to find an Iraqi connection to 9/11. There was none. Usually, a government ties its policy to the facts on the ground. In Bush's case, the policy was already set. The Plan for Invasion of Iraq in 2003 goes back to the Wolfowitz Plan in 1992 and the 1998 letter by the *Project for a New American Century.*

Since the policy was set to force regime change in Iraq, Bush manufactured facts on WMD to conform to the established policy. Cheney and his Chief of Staff "Scooter" Libby drove to CIA headquarters in Langley, Virginia, and instructed CIA Analysts as to what facts they had to find to support a finding of WMD.

In a weaker moment, CIA Director Tenet reportedly told Bush that finding Weapons of Mass Destruction (WMD) in Iraq would be a *"slam dunk"*. The minute Cheney and Libby walked through the front door of CIA Headquarters to *dictate* facts, **Tenet's days as CIA Director were numbered**.

Where was the *Horror of Hannity* while Bush and Cheney corrupted the very purpose of the CIA by telling analysts what facts to find? Hannity and Limbaugh only criticize Democrats. *Fair and Balanced* is the motto. Trump wants to disqualify Hillary because of some emails and the deaths of four brave Americans at Benghazi at the hands of terrorists.

Bush and Cheney caused the death of up to a hundred thousand, including nearly 6,000 Americans in Iraq and Afghanistan, and the *Horror of Hannity* sees only four dead Americans killed by terrorists at the U.S. Mission at Benghazi, Libya.

The only reason Trump and Hannity want to look at the Terrorist Raid on the U.S. Mission in Benghazi, Libya, is that Hillary was Secretary of State at the time. Since Trump is not qualified to be President, the Right Wing is desperate to disqualify Hillary. After multiple other investigations, Trey Gowdy and the Select Committee on Benghazi found Hillary *not* culpable for the death of four brave Americans at Benghazi.

After going down every possibility of disqualifying Hillary, and finding only Breitbart rumors of frail health, Hannity was desperate. Hannity and Jason Chaffetz wanted the FBI to recommend prosecution of Hillary for extreme sloppiness in handling sensitive emails at State. Director

Comey declined. Chaffetz, looking for a miracle, asked Comey to please arrange to indict Hillary for lying to Congress.

If Trump is not fit to serve as President, and if Hillary looks electable, the GOP must invent a pretext to disqualify her. The last and weakest straw is the rumor of health problems spread by the boys in the fever swamp at *Breitbart News and Views from the Dark Side*. What is frightening is that Trump brought in Stephen Bannon, Breitbart Chair, as CEO of the Trump Campaign.

The *Horror of Hannity* tries to make the rumors from the fever swamp fair and balanced news. Our Nation is a Democratic Republic, which has a detailed plan of succession in the event the President is unable or unwilling to serve.

The Vice President is first to succeed, followed by the Speaker of the House, President *pro tempore* of the Senate, and Members of the President's Cabinet according to date of establishment of the Department they head. There is no reason for voters to panic over perceived health issues. Hillary's health issues do not make Trump qualified to be President.

Jason Chaffetz wants to use the Clinton Foundation as a weight to sink Hillary's Campaign, or to try to delegitimize her Presidency if she wins. Chaffetz whined on CBS' *The Nation* on August 28, 2016, that someone should investigate conflicts of interest between the Clinton Foundation and the Clintons. What Chaffetz knows, but does not discuss, is that the organization established by Bill and Hillary is a **Public Charity**, not a Private Foundation. *Bill, Hillary, and Chelsea are not on the payroll of the Charity.*

The Charity has a Board of Directors. When Bill Clinton steps down as a Director, the Clintons will have no direct influence over the Charity. Chaffetz and the *Horror of Hannity* are desperately grasping at potential conflicts of interest with the Charity as a last ditch effort to stop Hillary, or to support an ongoing investigation if she is elected.

The best way to deal with Jason Chaffetz is for the Good People of Utah to vote him out of office.

The Nation will be ill served if Republicans in Congress spend another four or eight years trying to delegitimize a popularly elected president.

Chapter 7
Hannity Is Un-American

The American Way is to have a vigorous, honest debate based on facts. Trump and Hannity have abandoned facts to hide in the shadow of lies, smears, and bull. According to Lawrence O'Donnell, one writer observed that a bull artist is worse than a liar. A liar leaves bright lines of demarcation that are vulnerable to refutation. The bull artists, like Trump, Gingrich, Giuliani, and Christie, leave the lines of separation blurry, where confusion protects the bunkum.

Donald Trump has a record of discriminating against African American housing applicants The Justice Department brought an enforcement action against Trump under the *Fair Housing Act*. Trump entered into a Consent Judgment, denying liability but promising not to violate the Act again.

Trump has taken positions hostile Moslems, Minorities, Hispanics, and Mexicans. In a desperate attempt to confuse the issue, Trump accused Hillary of being a bigot. Trump is a warlord to thirty million angry white men.

Trump is an expert liar, but he is also an expert at bull. Trump hopes to hide in the confusion where he blurs the line between truth, lies, and bull. Abraham Lincoln was right. *'You cannot fool all of the People all of the time.'*

The poll numbers show that the People are on to Trump as a master of lies and bull. Trump has already prepared his swan song. *"The system is rigged".* This is a pathetic dog whistle aimed at the boys in the fever swamp at *Breitbart News and Views from the Dark Side* and at Trump's rabid Right Wing supporters. The system is supposed to expose liars and bull artists. The system is doing exactly what it is supposed to do.

The *Horror of Hannity* is that he is Un-American. If Hannity were a believer in the American way of life, he would have raised questions about Trump's anti American rants and policies. Hannity makes $22 million a year supporting whoever turns up as the GOP Candidate. Trump is the GOP Candidate.

Therefore, Trump can do no wrong in Hannity's eyes. The final straw was Trump's appointment of Stephen Bannon, Chair of *Breitbart News and Views from the Dark Side* as CEO of the Trump Campaign. Hannity knows that Hillary is more qualified than Trump to be President.

That is why Hannity is desperate to disqualify Hillary over emails, over Benghazi, over the Clinton Foundation, over anything. Trey Gowdy (R-SC), Chair of the *Select Benghazi Committee,* was supposed to bring Hillary down. The FBI was supposed to disqualify Hillary over the emails she sent at State. Nothing seemed to work in the Republicans' favor.

Desperate for some way to disqualify Hillary, the *Horror of Hannity* has embraced the bobble head syndrome disqualifier. Hannity aired a video of Hillary bobbing her head in response to a flurry of reporters' questions asked all at once. Hannity and his quack doctors feel that Hillary had a stroke or some other kind of disabling event. At all events, who would want to vote for a bobble head for president?

Wouldn't you rather have a pathological liar and bull artist extraordinaire in the White House.? Of course, Hannity and Trump were excited when Hillary had to leave the 9/11 commemoration in New York early, and her doctor later diagnosed pneumonia. Hillary's illness does not make Donald Trump qualified.

Chapter 8
Eight More Years of Whitewater?

Bill Clinton won the election in 1992. The Clintons had made an investment along with some other people in a tract of Arkansas land known as Whitewater. The developers borrowed money from Madison Guaranty Savings & Loan, a federally insured lender. When Madison Guaranty failed, the Resolution Trust Company (failed Savings & Loan receiver) wanted to recover lost funds.

Since the President and First Lady were investors in Whitewater, it became politically expedient to accuse the Clintons of some ill-defined wrongdoing. President Clinton made a **gross mistake**. Bill Clinton requested a Special Prosecutor to clear his name. What followed was a seven-year investigation that had no desire to end. The Clinton's would forever regret their mistake.

Attorney General Janet Reno initially appointed Robert Fiske Special Prosecutor. After the Special

Prosecutor law passed, the U.S. Court of Appeals for the District of Columbia Circuit appointed Kenneth Starr, a retired appellate court judge. The Court mandate limited the scope of the investigation.

The original mandate was to investigate Whitewater, and whether the Clintons were culpable for the failure of Madison Guaranty. The Special Prosecutor found nothing to implicate the Clintons. Vince Foster, a friend and aide to the President, committed suicide. The Special Prosecutor investigated the death of Vince Foster on the tenuous theory that Vince Foster may have known something about Whitewater, and someone may have wanted to make sure he did not disclose what he knew. No evidence appeared concerning foul play in Vince Foster's death.

The Special Prosecutor had nothing to do, so he investigated the White House Travel Office. There seemed to be no rationale to investigate the Travel Office, other than to tie the President up in an endless investigation. The Special Prosecutor, his team of attorneys, and their investigators found no evidence to implicate the Clintons in the failure of Madison Guaranty.

Travelgate was a dry hole. Filegate fizzled out. Starr reviewed Whitewater and the death of Vince Foster. The Office of Special Prosecutor could not find any evidence implicating the Clintons. Starr was bored. Starr **resigned** to become Dean of Pepperdine Law School.

The Right Wing raised a Firestorm of protest. How dare Ken Starr resign while Clinton was still president? Ken Starr put Pepperdine on hold. Starr withdrew his resignation. There was, however, nothing left to investigate under the Court's mandate, as revised. The lawsuit by Paula Jones raised questions about Bill Clinton's extracurricular activity.

There were questions about an affair with a White House Intern. Starr, as Chief Voyeur, actually went back to the D.C. Court of Appeals to ask if he could look at sex as the Whitewater Special Prosecutor. Being Republicans, and not wishing any peace to the Clintons, the Court of Appeals Panel of three judges turned Starr loose.

After finding Monica Lewinski's pristine Blue Dress that never made it to the cleaners, Starr submitted a Special Prosecutor's Report. Starr did not submit facts without making gratuitous legal conclusions. Starr submitted a **Brief for Impeachment** of the President. Right Wing zealots in the House happily obliged. The House Impeached for High Crimes and Misdemeanors, namely, for falsehood under oath denying the affair and obstruction of the Special Prosecutor. The Senate reluctantly heard the sordid accusations, and failed to convict. Having done half his job, Starr went on to Malibu, California, as Dean of Pepperdine Law School.

Twenty years later, in May 2016, Starr had to resign as President of Baylor University for failing to take seriously rape charges made by students against members of the Baylor Football Team. It seems that none of the complainants accused a Democratic president, or there was nothing for Starr to gain by bringing popular athletes within the purview of the law. In August 2016, Starr resigned as Law Professor, severing all ties with Baylor.

The *Horror of Hannity* is that Hannity wants to have a repeat of a seven-year investigation if Hillary wins the election. If the boys in the fever swamp and the *Talking Heads* cannot disqualify Mrs. Clinton, and she wins the election, the Right Wing in Congress can try to tie up her presidency in investigations. That is why it is important for the Democrats to take back the House and Senate.

Hannity maintains that Whitewater and the death of Vince Foster are **open chapters**, along with the Clinton Charity. Jason Chaffetz cannot wait to begin the permanent investigation of **President** Hillary. The handwriting is on the wall. Take back the House and Senate, American Voters, or waste another seven or eight years of Republican Congressional attacks on the Clintons and the Clinton Charity.

Chapter 9
Take Back the House and Senate

Congress enacted the *Affordable Care Act* (ACA) in 2010, when Democrats controlled the House, Senate, and White House. Not one Republican in either chamber voted for the ACA. The boycott was unusual because Universal Health Care with an Individual Mandate was a long time **Republican idea** that went back to Richard Nixon's days in the White House. The Heritage Foundation, a conservative *'Think Tank'*, supported the idea in the 1990s. Mitt Romney implemented Universal Health Care in Massachusetts in 1994. Romney relied on advice from Professor Gruber at MIT.

Romney wrote an Op-Ed recommending Romney Care as a model for a national health care plan. Everything went swimmingly, until President Obama touched the Republican idea. Obama took Romney's advice and based the federal healthcare plan on Romney Care. President Obama also relied upon Professor Gruber, and drew from the Massachusetts Plan. Republicans universally rejected the ACA because President Obama touched it.

At first, the GOP Party Line was *'Repeal and Replace'* the ACA. Four years later, it was *'Repeal'*, because Republicans had nothing to offer as a replacement health care plan. Some GOP stalwarts offered *'ACA Light'*. They borrowed the best features from the ACA, such as eliminating exclusion of coverage based on preexisting condition, and allowing children to remain on parent's policies until age 26.

From 2013 to 2016, Republicans passed more than 50 bills to repeal, defund, or otherwise **cripple** the ACA. If Donald trump is elected President, the Congress likely will repeal the ACA. It is essential that Democrats take back the Senate in 2016 and take back a number of House Seats. Without control of the Congress, progressive legislation will be stymied. Since the Census of 2010, the Republicans have taken unfair advantage of their control of about thirty state governments. GOP legislators gerrymandered districts to control the House and state legislatures.

Republicans have sold their birthright for a bowl of porridge. In the land of the brave and the home of the free, the GOP has a policy of suppressing votes. What good is the Fourteenth Amendment if states, north and south, use resources to deny minorities a chance to vote without waiting in line for four to six hours. It is a national disgrace that the GOP suppresses minority votes.

Chapter 10
The Great Non Debate

On September 7, 2016, there was no debate in the traditional sense. The two candidates for president were not on the same stage together. NBC and Matt Lauer presented a Commander-in-Chief Open Forum staged on the deck of the U.S.S. Intrepid. One searched in vain for the banner, **'Mission Accomplished'**, but, of course, nothing much was accomplished. Trump's audience had the same question.

Which of these two candidates is more unqualified, or disqualified? By not defending her use of a home server for State Department emails, Hillary Clinton took a giant step toward putting the controversy behind her. She said she was wrong, and would not do it again. Then came an interesting assertion. According to Mrs. Clinton, none of the documents involved contained the usual stamp or header "Top Secret", "Secret", or "Confidential".

 If so, this would seem to make the controversy over emails less of a make or break issue. The FBI reportedly found that within the body of some of the email documents, there was a "(c)" in the text on some pages to indicate that what followed, such as a telephone number or other sensitive data, was confidential. One wonders if Mrs. Clinton's handling of State Department emails really put the Nation at risk as claimed by the GOP.

 Matt Lauer instructed the candidates not to attack the other at the Commander-in-Chief Forum. In Trump's case, it seemed that Lauer cautioned not to attack *"too much"*. The Forum would not make many voters change their positions. As usual, Trump was short on details of his plans for *"taking the country back"*. Trump claims that he does not want to give America's enemies [or voters] advance knowledge of what he would do in any particular situation.

 Trump praised the U.S. military but expressed doubts about the generals who are advising President Obama. Trump wants to undermine the Obama Administration and Hillary Clinton as a former key member of the Administration. In the meantime, President Obama's approval rating is near 53%. Trump's is near 43%, with his negatives well over 50%. If the 2016 Election is a Popularity Contest, Trump has done almost everything he could do to make himself unpopular with most groups.

Hispanics are the fastest growing group in the country, and comprise about 15% of the vote. African Americans comprise about 12%. Women are 51%. Trump has needlessly alienated most of these groups. Trump's message to African Americans is, **"What do you have to lose?"**

Trump wants to double his poll numbers with blacks. He may be successful. He may take 2% of the black vote. In desperation, Trump is now visiting black churches. When Meghan Kelly asked Trump why he insulted women, he suggested that she was out to get him. In a bizarre rant he said, *"Blood was coming out of her eyes, out of her wherever"*.

There seem to be at least two Donald Trumps. One is a highly competitive businessperson, who exaggerates his success and his wealth. The other is a petulant teenager, who is narcissistic, short tempered, and disrespectful of authority. Is Trump still lashing out at his father for sending the 15 year old to the confinement of a military school?

Voters cannot take the adult Mr. Trump without getting the petulant teenage Donald. As a sign of the demographic collapse of the Trump Campaign, he is not the overwhelming favorite of Republicans. The boys in the fever swamp cannot get enough of Trump and *Breitbart News and Views from the Dark Side*. However, the gentle woman in Peoria and the gentle man in Birmingham are not persuaded that Trump is the answer.

Hispanics and conservatives feel betrayed by Trump's flip flopping on immigration. He is obviously pandering to both groups. Trump realizes that he cannot win without more than 22% of the Hispanic vote. He knows cannot win without two-third or more of the conservative vote. He claims he is not a politician, but he talks from both sides of his mouth.

At the end of the day, voters will choose the person they feel is most qualified. Based on experience, that person is Hillary Clinton. Republicans do not claim that she is not qualified. They claim she is disqualified. The GOP cites three topics to disqualify Mrs. Clinton. The first is the use of a home server and sloppiness in handing State Department emails.

There is no *'smoking gun'*, however, in the email controversy. Voters are not likely to rule out someone because they did not follow the correct procedure when they re-issued an email with a "(c)" in the text of one or more pages. The documents did not have a Stamp or **Header** on the front page to indicate that it contained Classified Information, which raises questions about how serious at all the information in the email was.

If Hillary re-issued the email, the "(c)" would be there in any event, and Mrs. Clinton would not have changed the security classification of the document.

The next issue the GOP suggests to disqualify Mrs. Clinton is that she was Secretary of State at the time terrorists attacked the U.S. Mission at Benghazi, Libya, and killed four brave American officials. Congress and the State Department conducted five investigations of the Benghazi attack.

There is no evidence that Mrs. Clinton is culpable for the deaths of the four brave Americans lost at Benghazi or that she gave a stand down order to the Department of Defense or anyone else to call off any rescue effort. Republicans were furious that Susan Rice, Security Advisor, to President Obama, tried to explain the Benghazi attack as a reaction to an anti Moslem video distributed by a pastor in California.

Rice appeared on the Sunday Talk Shows after the incident, and briefed based on *Talking Points* she received. The CIA appears to have had a hand in revising the *Talking Points*, because one of the villas the terrorists attacked in Benghazi was run by the CIA.

What *lessons learned* came out of Benghazi. (1). That when Congress makes cuts to State Department Budget requests for Security for American Facilities throughout the world, some facilities are not going to be as secure as they would have been. (2). That an American Mission in an unstable area overseas, consisting of unprotected villas that are not co-located or protected by perimeter walls, is vulnerable to attack.

Ambassador Chris Stevens wanted to be in Benghazi despite the danger, because that is where the action was. The rebellion against Ghaddafi got its spark in Benghazi. The CIA doubtless wanted its section of the U.S. Mission operating because of the information that it could obtain in Benghazi.

Republicans were not satisfied with the results of seven previous investigations of the Benghazi attack. The GOP turned to Trey Gowdy (R-SC) in a last ditch effort to disqualify Hillary Clinton. The U.S. House of Representatives appointed Gowdy Chair of a Select Committee to investigate Benghazi for the fifth time. Gowdy was an experienced state and federal prosecutor.

Gowdy promised that the Hearing would be a Trial. The defendant, of course, was Hillary Clinton. She testified for a record of 11 hours on one day before a panel dominated by hostile Republicans, who were at times rude and crude. One Right Winger asked Mrs. Clinton where she was later in the night of the Benghazi attack after she left her office at State. Mrs. Clinton said, *"I went to bed"*. The Lady Republican on the Select Committee asked, *"Were you alone?"*

The last great alleged scandal the Republicans are celebrating is the potential conflict of interest between the Clintons and the Clinton Charity. GOP wheeler dealers do not want the Clintons to enjoy the Pay for Play lifestyle that Republicans covet for themselves. The Clintons do not receive remuneration from the Clinton Charity. The Clintons, instead, receive world acclaim for the good works of the Clinton Charity. This drives Clinton haters like Jason Chaffetz and Trey Gowdy nuts.

There is no quid pro quo to prosecute. It really does not matter if Bill Clinton resigns as a Director of the Clinton Charity. If the Charity continues to do good work, the Clintons will receive praise and thanks across the globe.

Chapter 11
George W. Bush's Mess

The *Horror of Hannity* is that Hannity refuses to talk about the **Elephant in the Room**. All we hear about is that President Obama allegedly should have made more of a surge in military force, or more surges, or both, in Iraq and Afghanistan. Senators John McCain (R-AZ) and Lindsey Graham (R-SC) wear nothing but Red, White, and Blue Serge Suits. Hannity does not want to talk about the *Elephant in the Room*. The plain truth is that George W. Bush created and abandoned the **Mess in Iraq**.

It is wonderful that Bush is a born again Christian. That, however, made him susceptible to the crusade promoted by the Christian militants. The Neoconservatives joined forces with the Christian militants to forge a disastrous plan to Invade Iraq. *'Regime Change'* was the password to traipse through the looking glass darkly. Hawks in Congress want President Obama to step up military action in Iraq, and to increase the U.S. 'training force' in Afghanistan.

The only authorization by Congress for use of military force in Iraq and Afghanistan dates to 2002-2003. GOP hawks in Congress **refused** President Obama's request for an updated war resolution in 2015-2016. Ditto for the president's request for a resolution on Syria. John McCain and Lindsey Graham want President Obama to use the U.S. military to stop the carnage of the civil war in Syria. Congress, however, has the power under the Constitution to declare war.

The GOP dominated Congress refuses to pass a bill on U.S. military action in Syria. Some GOP critics want Obama to impose a **No Fly Zone** over Syria. With Russian war planes actively engaged in Syria, a No Fly Zone would require the cooperation of Vladimir Putin, President of Russia. The chaos in Syria is directly caused by the misadventure of the Bush Cheney Administration in Iraq.

Neoconservatism goes back to changes in political thinking in the 1930s, when academics began to doubt the bona fides of Marxism. Gradually, the old left drifted toward conservatism. They became the Neoconservatives. Professor Leo Strauss (University of Chicago) was the inspiration. Wolfowitz took some courses with Strauss. Irving Krystol was the Godfather of the movement.

William Kristol, the son, publishes the *Weekly Standard*. Neocons wanted to take advantage of America's strength as the only superpower after the dissolution of the Soviet Union in 1991. Neocons wanted to flex America's muscles.

In 1998, Neocons, under the banner of the **Project for a New American Century**, wrote a letter to President Bill Clinton to urge **Regime Change** in Iraq. Paul Wolfowitz had been advocating for removal of Saddam Hussein for years. The idea of removing Saddam Hussein from power caught on as well with Christians and with Jews.

Christians imagined a battle of Good versus Evil taking place on the plains of Megiddo in northern Israel, or in Baghdad. Jews were willing to join if it meant the end of Saddam Hussein. Neocons were thrilled at the prospect. Into this volatile mix wandered an optimistic, born again Christian named George W. Bush.

Ironically, Poppy Bush, led a coalition in 1990 to force Saddam out of Kuwait. Neocons, Dick Cheney, as then Secretary of Defense, and George W., were disappointed that Poppy Bush did not topple Saddam in 1990-91. Rumor had it that Saddam was behind a plot to assassinate Poppy Bush.

From day one of his presidency, George W. planned to topple Saddam. Paul O'Neil, Bush's first Secretary of Commerce, recalls that the first cabinet meeting discussed the Saddam problem. Paul Wolfowitz, Undersecretary of Defense, was an independent voice for *Regime Change* in Iraq.

Bush gave little or no attention to Osama bin Laden, though bin Laden was responsible for a truck bomb attack against the Word Trade Center in **1993**, simultaneous bombings of the U.S. Embassies in Nairobi, Kenya, and Dar Es Salaam, Tanzania, in **1998**, and the attack against the U.S.S. Cole in **2000**.

While Bush was thinking about Regime Change in Iraq to restore the Bush family honor and to assuage the Neocons and Christian Crusaders, bin Laden launched the

9/11 attack from his sanctuary in Afghanistan. Bush's timetable for Iraq had to wait. Bush ordered the Taliban rulers in Kabul to hand over bin Laden. Taliban Leaders received large sums of money from bin Laden, and so refused to give him up.

The CIA took on the Taliban, and nearly caught bin Laden twice. The U.S. Army joined in to pacify Afghanistan. After a short bombing phase in Afghanistan, where the Air Force soon ran out of military targets, Bush turned his attention back to Regime Change in Iraq. There already was a Plan for the Invasion of Iraq, written by Paul Wolfowitz and Douglas Feith for Secretary of Defense Dick Cheney in 1992.

The reason everything was ready to go to war for the Neocons in the Bush Administration is that Cheney selected most of them. Bush asked Cheney to head the transition team in 2000. Cheney picked himself for Vice President, and Donald Rumsfeld as Secretary of Defense.

Cheney and Rumsfeld picked Wolfowitz and Feith. Cheney picked Powell for State. Cheney picked Neocons for key positions in State and Defense. Condi Rice was Security Advisor, and when Powell left, Condi became Secretary of State. Condi trained as a Soviet Expert, but was not an expert in handling problems in the Middle East.

WMD Propaganda

Bush, Cheney, Rumsfeld, Rice, and Wolfowitz knew that they must prepare (read, 'brainwash') the American People for War. You cannot just invade another country without good cause. The solution was to cast Saddam as a threat to use Weapons of Mass Destruction (WMD). Cheney corrupted the CIA by personally instructing analysts what they must find.

Then came the mantra, *'We do not want the first sign of WMD to be a mushroom cloud'*. The *Horror of Hannity* is that the GOP apologists never questioned the GOP Party Line. They led us into war on false pretenses. Bush sent David Kay and a team of weapons experts to Iraq to find WMD. After two years, David Kay reported, *'We were all wrong about WMD.'*

The Planning for the Invasion of Iraq was unrealistic. Rumsfeld imagined he could defeat the Iraqi Army, occupy and pacify Iraq with as few as 50,000 troops. After protest by the military, Rumsfeld increased the invasion force. When Poppy Bush planned to push Saddam out of Kuwait, he assembled a coalition force of 950,000 troops, including 700,000 U.S. troops.

Bush, Jr, did not have any plan for pacifying Iraq, establishing a new Iraqi Government, or turning government over to the Iraqis. At one time after the invasion, Wolfowitz thought he might go to Baghdad to govern Iraq. Instead, Bush sent State Department's L. Paul ("Jerry") Bremer to act as Head of Coalition Provisional Authority.

The Third Infantry Division and the Marines did an outstanding job of neutralizing the Iraqi Army. Some of the Iraqi Air Force flew to Iran to hide. After the fall of the Iraqi armed forces, there was a lull in military activity and civilian opposition. It gradually dawned on Iraqis, however, that there was no government. The U.S. did not send the number of troops required.

The Iraqi people started looting museums and government offices. U.S. Troops did nothing. Secretary of Defense Rumsfeld's response was, *"Stuff Happens."* Indeed, a lot of bad stuff happened on Rumsfeld's watch. After the looting, the real damage started. The U.S. sparked an

Insurrection by imposing dubious occupation policies. The Coalition Provisional Authority (CPA) brought about the Iraq Insurgency.

L. Paul Bremer, presumptively carrying out directions from Wolfowitz and Rumsfeld, issued **CPA Order #1**, which prohibited Ba'athist Party Members, down to the third level, from obtaining meaningful military or civilian jobs in the new Iraq. Bremer followed with **CPA Order #2**, which disbanded the Iraqi Army.

This meant that there would be hundreds of thousands of disgruntled Iraqis roaming the streets and looking for a way to repay the U.S. Many of the dissidents were ex-military, and able to find weapons easily. Bremer was in a unique position. He was the personal emissary of President Bush, so he could talk with the president.

He was supposed to report to Don Rumsfeld, so Wolfowitz and the Pentagon could have his ear. Condi Rice was Security Advisor to the President, so she frequently contacted Bremer personally. At one point, Rumsfeld must have seen a disaster in the making. In one conversation, Condi Rice mentioned that Bremer worked for Rumsfeld. Rumsfeld bailed, saying, *'No, he works for you'.* Rumsfeld no longer wanted responsibility for Bremer and the CPA.

Flowers, Chocolate, and Cakewalk Myth

Paul Wolfowitz preached the false doctrine that the Iraqis would greet the U.S. Third Infantry Division and Marine invaders with *Flowers and Chocolate*. The rationale of the Neocons was that Saddam was a brutal dictator, and the U.S. Military were Liberators.

Most of the civilian management team at the Pentagon believed this fable. Ken Adelman was an assistant to Donald Rumsfeld during the first tour of duty as Secretary of Defense under Gerald Ford. Adelman was a Neocon and

supporter of the **Project for a New American Century**.
Adelman wrote editorials in the *Washington Post* in support
of the 2003 Invasion of Iraq.

"I believe that demolishing Hussein's military power
and liberating Iraq would be a **cakewalk**." 2/02 (bolding
added).

"My confidence 14 months ago sprang from having
worked for Don Rumsfeld three times —knowing he would
fashion a most creative and detailed war plan—and from
knowing Dick Cheney and Paul Wolfowitz well for many
years." 4/03

Adelman later expressed regrets in *Vanity Fair*.11/06

"I just presumed that what I considered to be the most
competent national security team since Truman was indeed
going to be competent. They turned out to be among the
most incompetent teams in the postwar era. Not only did
each of them, individually, have enormous flaws, but
together they were deadly, dysfunctional." Borgia, Julia,
The Guardian 11/4/06.

There *was* a bit of cheering in Baghdad when the U.S.
and locals pulled down the statue of Saddam. When Iraqi's
realized, however, that there was no effective
government—that Bush, Rumsfeld, Wolfowitz, and Bremer
lacked the resources and the will to control Iraq— they
resorted to their equivalent of 2nd Amendment Remedies.

L. Paul Bremer was dictator in Iraq, just like Saddam
Hussein a year earlier. There was on major difference.
Bremer did not control security. The U.S. military had
security forces. Bremer did not control how much money
he would receive to run his empire.

In short, Bremer was a paper tiger. None of the
planners of the Invasion understood the deep sectarian and
ethnic divisions in Iraq. Iraq was not a true nation. Iraq was

an invention of British mapmakers after World War I. Iraq was a remnant of the dissolved Ottoman Empire. For centuries before, however, Mesopotamia (the land between the rivers Tigris and Euphrates) existed as three autonomous city-states. Mosul in the north, Baghdad in the middle, and Basra in the south. Iraq was never a nation.

George W. Bush's problem is that he knew little about the Iraqi population. Bush did not know the difference between a Shia, a Sunni, or a Kurd. Bush's Security Advisor, Condi Rice, was a Soviet Expert. Saddam Hussein was a dictator, who ruled Iraq on behalf of the Sunnis.

The Sunnis suppressed the Shia majority. After the U.S. pushed Saddam out of Kuwait in 1991, The Shia thought they had a green light from the U.S. to overthrow Saddam. The Shia organized a rebellion in the marsh area. Saddam sent his military in to slaughter the Shia rebels. Poppy Bush did not lift a finger to protect the Shia rebels. When the Third Infantry and the Marines arrived in 2003, the Shia were not the rebels they were in 1991.

One reason that Poppy Bush did not turn the tanks west in 1990, and invade Baghdad, was that he had concerns that the dissolution of Iraq could destabilize the entire Middle East. The Sunnis comprise only about 20% of the Iraqi population. The Kurds in the north and the Shia make up most of the balance.

The Kurds have significant adjoining populations in Syria, Iraq, Iran, Turkey, and parts of the old Soviet Union If Iraq were to dissolve, the Kurds would try to establish their own homeland. This would have a devastating effect on Turkey, a key U.S. and NATO ally. Turkey has fought Kurdish rebels for years. Poppy Bush had a global and regional understanding not matched by his swashbuckling son.

In the past, the U.S. used Iraq as a counterforce to Iran. Both countries are predominately Shia Moslem. Saddam Hussein, however, suppressed the Shia, and placed Sunnis in control of Iraq. This made Iraq a natural enemy of Iran under Saddam. The U.S. was fully capable of managing Saddam. By toppling Saddam, the U.S. handed Iran a great victory.

The Shia government in Iraq is under the influence of the Shia government in Iran. The Ayatollah never dreamed that the U.S. would do his work for him. To help Iran gain hegemony over Iraq, the U.S. sacrificed nearly 6,000 military and spent nearly two trillion dollars. The irony is that Iraq had nothing to do with the al Qaeda attack on the U.S. on 9/11.

The *Horror of Hannity* blames Obama and Hillary for the spread of ISIS, the Islamic State. Hannity will say that Obama pulled out of Iraq too soon, and reduced troop levels too fast. George W. Bush, however, set the date for U.S. departure from Iraq. The U.S. required a *Status of Forces Agreement*, granting immunity to U.S. troops. The Iraqis refused to sign the agreement. When the Iraqis also refused Obama's request for a *Status of Forces Agreement*, Obama merely implemented the timetable set by Bush for draw down of U.S. troops in Iraq.

George W. Bush let the genie out of the bottle in 2003, and could not clean up his own mess by January 20, 2009. The *Horror of Hannity* refuses to acknowledge the mess George W. Bush made.

Donald Rumsfeld does not always admit that he sent too few troops to Iraq. Rumsfeld claims that his Commander on the Ground, General Tommy Franks, told Rumsfeld he did not need any more troops. If so, Franks was not properly briefed on his Mission, or the Mission was ill defined. The Mission had to be more than to topple Saddam. The mission should have been to defeat the Iraqi military, enforce law and order, and to secure Iraqi borders.

Iraq shares a border of hundreds of miles with Syria, hundreds of miles with Iran, a lesser border with Saudi Arabia, and a short border with Jordan. How many troops would it take to secure seven hundred miles of Iraq's borders? At least 100,000. It is not known how many Jihadis drove their pick-up trucks between Damascus, Syria, and Baghdad, and Amman, Jordan, and Baghdad during the 2003 Iraq War.

General Shinseki was correct. The Army Chief of Staff counseled that it would take hundreds of thousands of U.S. Troops to invade and occupy Iraq. Bush and hi amateur civilians all thought they knew better than the professional soldiers.

Chapter 12
Voters Get What They Tolerate

Political Discourse seems to be at all-time low in the U.S. Donald Trump has made the crude and the vulgar into the routine. With use of juvenile epithets like *'Crooked Hillary'* and *'Lying Ted'*, Trump hit the bedrock of profane politicking. *'Low energy Jeb'* may not be obscene or hateful, but Trump intended to destroy his opponent with the turn of a phrase. Are progressives and even a number of Republicans fair, when they note that Trump does not always tell the truth?

Trump made it difficult to have the perquisites of a normal politician, because he has trashed the truth continually. Trump became **Birther-in-Chief** in 2011, because playing that role was politically expedient. He knew President Obama was born in Hawaii, USA. Trump knew, however, that the boys in the fever swamp would follow him anywhere if he disrespected the first Black President in U.S. history.

To affirm his false accusation about Obama's birthplace, Trump announced that he would send investigators Hawaii to disprove the legitimacy of Obama's birth certificate. We are still waiting for the reports from Trump's investigators.

History shows that American politics always bristled with animosity and distrust. President Washington counseled against factions (parties). We were supposed to be one big, happy family. There was almost a Civil War, however, before there was a Nation. Federalists wanted a national government with the power to tax, to enact laws, to adjudicate *federal* claims in *federal* courts, and to wage war, if necessary.

Anti Federalists wanted to preserve States' Rights Sovereignty Two sovereigns cannot reign over the same locale. George Mason would rather cut off his hand than put it to the Constitution as proposed. The only way to have a country was to compromise. George Washington was appointed Commander of the Continental Army during the Revolution and was the universal choice for first president because he was from Virginia. The capital moved from New York to Philadelphia to the District of Columbia to be closer to the South.

The political bickering was more ferocious in the beginning than it is today. Everyone pretended that there were no factions (parties), to keep Washington content. Behind the scenes, Hamilton's Federalists and banking interests were plotting against Jefferson's state's rights and agrarian interests. They accused Hamilton of plotting to bring back the monarchy. Personal feuds settled by dueling with pistols.

On July 11, 1804, Aaron Burr shot Alexander Hamilton at Weehawken, New Jersey, over a perceived insult. It might have been Burr and Jefferson dueling, because they hated each other. Burr and Jefferson tied in the Electoral College vote in 1800. Burr insisted that he should be President. Most understood that Jefferson was the intended president.

Usually, the electors would make sure that the candidate intended for President received at least one more Electoral Vote than the candidate for Vice President. In 1800, someone did not get the message. Since no one had an Electoral majority, the House had to vote to break the tie.

The House of Representatives selected Jefferson in 1801 after 36 ballots. The result was an Administration with Jefferson as President, and Burr as Vice President, where the two were not on speaking terms. It took a Constitutional Amendment (# 12) to make sure the standoff did not occur again. Electors in future elections had to specify that one vote was for president and the other for vice president. The Election Ticket would show which candidate was supposed to be President and which the Vice President.

The President and Vice President could have the same number of Electoral Votes, but it was clear who should be President. If the Vice President somehow received more votes than the President, the Vice President would still be only Vice President.

The election of 1800 was significant in that it marked the end of the Federalist Party as a viable political party. The federalists won the day in 1789, with the approval of a federal constitution. Washington took the presidency from 1789-1797 Washington claimed he did not belong to a political party. Effectively, however, he was a federalist. John Adams was the last federalist president, serving one term, from 1797-1801.

By 1804, Hamilton, the Federalist Leader, would be dead from a duel with Aaron Burr. The election of 1800 was personal, dirty, and full of accusations. Federalists smeared Jefferson by suggesting that his pro-French policy might bring the excesses of the French Revolution to the U.S. Hamilton plotted against his fellow federalist, because he thought Adams resisted adopting some of Hamilton's proposed policies.

Jefferson supporters accused federalists of subverting the Republic with the passage of the Alien & Sedition Laws, which (1) was the first anti immigrant law in the U.S., and (2) criminalized criticism of the federal government.

Donald Trump would have fit in nicely with the vituperative campaigns of 1796 and 1800. Trump's threat to deport 11 million undocumented workers is comparable to the exclusion provisions enacted by the Federalist in Congress in 1796 and 1800. They thought of themselves as the true, blue Americans. Jefferson's people were the foreigners because they seemed to favor the French.

Campaign Reform Vital

It is impossible to reform the character of Political Campaigns through legislation that would try to prohibit *'taking the low road'*. The First Amendment protects Freedom of Speech, a Free Press, and Freedom of Religion. *De Gustibus Non Est Disputandum*. Some may think that Donald Trump is vulgar and insulting. Others may think that Hillary is not trustworthy (as GOP Propaganda broadcasts 24/7). There is no law to correct the character or campaign style of a politician.

Voters can do the most to clean up political campaigns by rewarding the good and punishing the bad. Voters, however, are subject to manipulation and advertising campaigns. Ask anyone what they think of negative campaign advertising. The answer is always the same. Everyone condemns negative ads. Nevertheless, negative ads can stampede voters into making a wrong decision. There is no lawful way to stop negative ads, except for the public to vote in support of the target of the ad.

Usually it is not evident who is running the ad. An ad may be sponsored by groups with harmless or patriotic sounding names, such as *'Americans for Good Government',* or *'Americans for Progress',* or *Americans for Prosperity* (a Coke Brothers' front). If an ad is against a policy or regulation, that is a clue to sponsorship. The Coke Brothers run an industrial empire with a heavy carbon footprint.

They consider environmental protection laws and regulation an unnecessary or unfair burden on their business profits. They want to eliminate the Environmental Protection Agency (U.S. and state). The Coke Brothers vote for Libertarians or Republicans, who will try to keep government small. If government is small, government services should be, less according to conservative theory. If government services are less, taxes will be lower. The logic is linear and obvious. The ads on their face are not always traceable to the real party in interest.

The U.S. Supreme Court struck a blow for tyranny by equating money with free speech. There are few limits on the quantity of speech allowed in a political campaign. The Court missed the point of imposing reasonable limits on money in campaigns. A democratic Republic cannot survive an unlimited amount of money dumped into political campaigns.

Sooner, rather than later, the voice of the people will disappear under a flood of money that the upper 1% flow into the campaign. Congress tried to limit campaign funding through legislation. The *McCain-Feingold Act* imposed reasonable limits on political contributions.

The Federal Election Commission (FEC) has the mandate but not the power to regulate campaign funding. The FEC often cannot act decisively because of its organic structure of having as Commissioners an equal number of Democrats to an equal number of Republicans.

The Republicans on the Supreme Court virtually destroyed regulation of campaign financing by its anti democratic decision in **Citizens United v FEC**. The Court protects Money as if it were Speech. If a handful of billionaires decide that a particular presidential candidate is good for billionaires, they can flood the country with virtually unlimited ads that are positive on their candidate and negative on the opponents.

After Justice Scalia died, the Supreme Court cannot resolve closely contested issues because of a possible 4 to 4 tie vote. President Obama nominated a qualified federal judge for the Supreme Court. Senate Majority Leader McConnell refused to set hearings for confirmation or rejection of the nominee.

McConnell thinks that there is a chance that Donald Trump will win the 2016 Election. Republicans are destroying our democratic Republic by suppressing the vote, gerrymandering election districts on the state and federal level, and applauding the unfortunate decision to equate money with Free Speech.

Every Seat in the House of Representatives is up for election every two years, along with one-third of the Senate Seats. Our Founders gave us a road map for a democratic Republic. Voting is the cure all for shoddy or oppressive government. *The Price of Liberty is Eternal Vigilance.*

Another quote from Benjamin Franklin is his answer to a question of what kind of government we have. **"A Republic, if we can keep it."** We will lose our Republic if we do not vote. Republicans have made it difficult to vote. Republicans drew distorted Election Districts to put a majority of Republicans in as many districts as possible.

This Republicans want to control a District by a slim majority of 51%. To minimize Democrat Seats, Republicans include 60% of Democrats in a District. It is time consuming to seek relief in the Courts.

What do Republican Leaders Think of Trump?

You have to consider the source of opinions on Trump. There are the Pay to Play camp followers like former New York City Mayor Rudy Giuliani and former House Speaker Newt Gingrich. They have companies that market goods or services that depend on having influence with the party in power. They appeared as sycophants at the Republican Convention in Cleveland.

Governor of Ohio John Kasich is not marketing goods or services, so he did not toady up to Trump at the GOP Convention. Former Secretary of Defense Robert Gates said that Trump is **'beyond repair'**. Colin Powell, former Chair of the Joint Chiefs of Staff said in private email that Trump is a **'National Disgrace'**.

The people who will benefit from a Trump win are willing to sell their soul to the devil. Republican National Committee Chair Reince Priebus comes to mind. House Speaker Paul Ryan is torn between his duty to the Nation and his job as Speaker. He criticized Trump's racist remarks, but is afraid to condemn Trump's candidacy for fear of losing a majority in the House of Representatives.

To some Republicans a Trump win means that money and influence will be plentiful. Giuliani and Gingrich do not care if Trump causes racial and ethnic animosity. They want to sell more products and services. A group of fifty security and national defense policy experts denounced the Trump Campaign. Most of them are Republicans.

Trump said he was not impressed by Senator John McCain, because the North Vietnamese shot down McCain's plane and imprisoned him for five years. McCain was in a tough primary and general election in Arizona, so he endorsed Trump. and Trump finally endorsed John McCain.

The Donald is not a genuine Republican. He is not a true Democrat. He is egocentric, idiosyncratic, and more interested in winning than in upholding party principles or adhering to an ideology. Trump should have run as an Independent. Even though that label is the fastest growing political identifier in the Nation, the history of Independent Candidates in the U.S. is that they were *'also rans'*.

Bernie Sanders ran as an Independent most of his adult life. In 2016, he ran for the nomination of the Democrats to be president. Trump would have been equally at home or out of place in the Democratic Party as in the Republican Party.

Trump presents himself as a disrupter of the status quo, a perfectly acceptable position. It is imperfect, however, when our erstwhile disrupter relies upon stirring racial and ethnic animosity to distinguish himself.

Final Thoughts

(1). A Nation must have viable borders, or it risks being overrun by outsiders.

(2). East Germany, North Korea, and the Soviet Union had the most secure borders.

(3). Slavery brought wealth to planters, shippers, and traders, and shame to the Nation.

(4). Promoting an underclass of residents, who live in the shadows, is a step toward slavery.

(5). Providing a Path to Citizenship for 11 million illegal immigrants will benefit the Nation.

(6). The East German Wall kept residents in, and was not designed to keep intruders out.

(7). Donald Trump now is trying to look presidential, thanks to Manager Kellyanne Conway.

(8). Trump still holds unhinged ideas, thanks to CEO Stephen Bannon and Breitbart News.

(9). The GOP smear machine is desperate to disqualify Hillary Clinton to save Trump.

(10). The **Horror of Hannity** is that Hannity broadcasts GOP smears as truth.

(11). The Courts in the world's leading democracy should stop suppression of votes and reverse gerrymandering control of state and federal election districts.

(12). The U.S. Supreme Court **crippled** democracy by wrongly equating money with speech.